BBQ COOK OUTS RECIPE BOOK

50 SMOKY & TENDER RECIPES

AVA ISLA

TABLE OF CONTENTS

INTRODUCTION

Welcome to the BBQ cookbook!

You're about to embark upon an adventure that is not only fun, but maybe even a little addicting. One thing's for sure, though: It's delicious!

You're new to grilling? You're afraid to light a barbecue? Well, have no fear. It's not as complicated as it looks. This book has got some recipes ready to go and some even call for indoor grilling!

What is BBQ?

Barbecue originated from the Caribbean word 'barbacoa', which is a native Indian structure used for smoking meats.

It's important to note that grilling and barbecuing are two different concepts. While grilling uses high and direct heat for quick cooks (think burgers, hot dogs, and steak), Barbecuing, on the other hand, requires indirect, consistent, low heat and longer cook times. Barbecuing also uses different types of smoke wood for an additional layer of flavour on top of the charcoal smoke. Meat used for BBQ is also tends to have a higher fat content, which provides tenderization and flavour over a long cooking time.

Tips to get you started:

- To avoid losing juices during turning, always flip your meat or vegetables using tongs or a spatula.

- Don't press down anything with a spatula while they're grilling! This squeezes out the juices.

- For great smoky flavour, soak some wood chips in water.

- To infuse grilled foods with herb essence, toss herbs directly onto the charcoal while you're grilling.

POULTRY

1. Cajun Patch Cock Chicken

Ingredients:

- 4-5 pounds of fresh or thawed frozen chicken
- 4-6 glasses of extra virgin olive oil
- Cajun Spice Lab 4 tablespoons or Lucile Bloody Mary Mix Cajun Hot Dry Herb Mix Seasoning

Directions:

Rub olive oil freely under and on the skin. Season chicken in all Directions: and apply directly to the meat under the skin.

Wrap the chicken in plastic wrap and place in the refrigerator for 3 hours to absorb the flavor.

Make chicken for 1.5 hours.

Place the chicken under a loose foil tent for 15 minutes before carving.

2. Yan's Grilled Quarters

Ingredients:

- 4 fresh or thawed frozen chicken quarters
- 4-6 glasses of extra virgin olive oil
- 4 tablespoons of Yang's original dry lab

Directions:

Cut off excess skin and fat chicken. Carefully peel the chicken skin and rub olive oil above and below each chicken skin.

In Jean's original dry lab, apply seasonings to the top and bottom of the skin and the back of the chicken house.

Wrap the seasoned chicken in plastic wrap and store refrigerated for 2-4 hours to absorb flavor.

Place chicken on grill and cook at 325 ° F for 1 hour.

3. Roasted Tuscan Thighs

Ingredients:

- 8 chicken thighs, with bone, with skin
- 3 extra virgin olive oils with roasted garlic flavor
- 3 cups of Tuscan or Tuscan seasoning per thigh

Directions:

Lightly rub olive oil behind and below the skin and thighs. A seasoning from Tuscan, seasoned on the skin of the thigh and the top and bottom of the back.

Wrap chicken thighs in plastic wrap, refrigerate for 1-2 hours, and allow time for flavor to be absorbed before roasting.

Depending on the grill of the Smoker, roast for 40-60 minutes until the internal Smoke Temperature of the thick part of the chicken thigh reaches 180 ° F. Place the roasted Tuscan thighs under a loose foil tent for 15 minutes before serving.

4. Teriyaki Smoked Drumstick

Ingredients:

- 3 cup teriyaki marinade and cooking sauce like Yoshida's original gourmet
- Poultry seasoning 3 tsp
- 1 tsp garlic powder
- 10 chicken drumsticks

Directions:

In a medium bowl, mix the marinade and cooking sauce with the chicken seasoning and garlic powder.

Put the drumstick in a marinade pan or 1-gallon plastic sealable bag and pour the marinade mixture into the drumstick. Refrigerate overnight.

Place the skin on the drumstick and, while the grill is preheating, hang the drumstick on a poultry leg and wing rack to drain the cooking sheet on the counter. If you do not have a poultry leg and feather rack, you can dry the drumstick by tapping it with a paper towel.

After 1 hour, raise the hole Smoke Temperature to 350 ° F and cook the drumstick for another 30-45 minutes until the thickest part of the stick reaches an internal Smoke Temperature of 180 ° F.

5. Smoked Bone In-Turkey Breast

Ingredients:

- 1 (8-10 pounds) boned turkey breast
- 6 tablespoons extra virgin olive oil
- 5 Yang original dry lab or poultry seasonings

Directions:

Rub or season carefully under the chest cavity, under the skin and on the skin.

Place the turkey breast in a V-rack for secure handling or place it directly on a grill grate with the breast up.

Rest the turkey breasts on the kitchen counter at room Smoke Temperature and preheat the Smoker grill.

Smoke the boned turkey breast directly in a V rack or grill at 225 ° F for 2 hours.

After 2 hours of hickory smoke, raise the pit Smoke Temperature to 325 ° F. Roast until the thickest part of the turkey breast reaches an internal Smoke Temperature of 170 ° F and the juice is clear.

Place the hickory smoked turkey breast under a loose foil tent for 20 minutes, then scrape the grain.

6. Smoked Whole Duck

Ingredients:

- 5 pounds whole duck (trimmed of any excess fat)
- 1 small onion (quartered)
- 1 apple (wedged)
- 1 orange (quartered)
- 1 tbsp freshy chopped parsley
- 1 tbsp freshly chopped sage
- $\frac{1}{2}$ tsp onion powder
- 2 tsp smoked paprika
- 1 tsp dried Italian seasoning

- 1 tbsp dried Greek seasoning
- 1 tsp pepper or to taste
- 1 tsp sea salt or to taste

Directions:

To make rub, combine the onion powder, pepper, salt, Italian seasoning, Greek seasoning and paprika in a mixing bowl.

Insert the orange, onion, and apple to the duck cavity. Stuff the duck with freshly chopped parsley and sage.

Season all sides of the duck generously with rub mixture.

Place the duck on the grill grate.

Roast for 2 to 21/2 hours, or until the duck skin is brown and the internal Smoke Temperature of the thigh reaches 160°F.

7. Chicken Tenders

Ingredients:

- 6 chicken tenders
- $\frac{1}{4}$ tsp granulated garlic (not garlic powder)
- $\frac{1}{4}$ tsp pepper
- 1 tsp paprika
- $\frac{1}{2}$ tsp kosher salt
- 1 tbsp olive oil
- 1 tbsp lemon juice
- 1 tsp Italian seasoning
- 1 tbsp chopped parsley

Directions:

In a large mixing bowl, combine the garlic, pepper, salt, lemon, Italian seasoning and paprika. Add the chicken tenders and toss to combine. Cover the bowl and refrigerate for 1 hour.

Remove the chicken tenders from the marinade and let them rest for 1 hour, until the tenders are at room temperature. Pat dry with paper towels

Arrange the chicken tenders onto the grill and grill 8 minutes, 4 minutes per side.

8. Thanksgiving Turkey

Ingredients:

- 2 cups butter (softened)
- 1 tbsp cracked black pepper
- 2 tsp kosher salt
- 2 tbsp freshly chopped rosemary
- 2 tbsp freshly chopped parsley
- 2 tbsp freshly chopped sage
- 2 tsp dried thyme
- 6 garlic cloves (minced)
- 1 (18 pound) turkey

Directions:

In a mixing bowl, combine the butter, sage, rosemary, 1 tsp black pepper, 1 tsp salt, thyme, parsley, and garlic.

Use your fingers to loosen the skin from the turkey.

Generously, Rub butter mixture under the turkey skin and all over the turkey as well. 4. Season turkey generously with herb mix. 5. Preheat the grill to 300°F with lid closed for 15 minutes.

Place the turkey on the grill and roast for about 4 hours, or until the turkey thigh Smoke Temperature reaches 160°F.

Remove the turkey from the grill and let it rest for a few minutes.

Cut into sizes and serve.

9. Spatchcock Smoked Turkey

Ingredients:

- 1 (18 pounds) turkey
- 2 tbsp finely chopped fresh parsley
- 1 tbsp finely chopped fresh rosemary
- 2 tbsp finely chopped fresh thyme
- ½ cup melted butter
- 1 tsp garlic powder
- 1 tsp onion powder
- 1 tsp ground black pepper
- 2 tsp salt or to taste
- 2 tbsp finely chopped scallions

Directions:

In a mixing bowl, combine the parsley, rosemary, scallions, thyme, butter, pepper, salt, garlic, and onion powder.

Rub butter mixture over all sides of the turkey.

Preheat your grill to HIGH (450°F) with lid closed for 15 minutes.

Place the turkey directly on the grill grate and cook for 30 minutes. Reduce Preferred Wood Pellet to 300°F and cook for an additional 4 hours.

Remove the turkey from the grill and let it rest for a few minutes.

Cut into sizes and serve.

10. Smoked Chicken Leg Quarters

Ingredients:

- 8 chicken leg quarters
- 2 tbsp olive oil
- 1 tsp salt or to taste
- $\frac{1}{2}$ tsp chili powder
- $\frac{1}{2}$ tsp paprika
- $\frac{1}{2}$ tsp ground thyme
- 1 tsp dried rosemary
- $\frac{1}{2}$ tsp cayenne pepper
- 1 tsp garlic powder
- 1 tsp onion powder

Directions:

To make rub, combine cayenne, rosemary, garlic, onion powder, chili, paprika, salt and thyme.

Drizzle oil over the chicken leg quarters and season the quarters generously with rub mix.

Arrange the chicken onto the grill grate. Smoke for 1 hour, flipping halfway through.

Cook for an additional 1 hour.

Remove chicken from grill and let it rest for about 15 minutes.

Serve and enjoy.

11. Lemon Garlic Smoked Chicken

Ingredients:

- Whole Chicken (3-lbs., 1.4-kg.)
- The Brine
- Salt – ½ cup
- Brown sugar – 1 cup
- Water – 3 ½ liters

The Rub

- Minced garlic – ¼ cup
- Garlic powder – 2 tablespoons
- Lemon juice – 3 tablespoons
- Paprika – 2 ½ tablespoons

- Chili powder – 2 tablespoons
- Thyme – ¾ tablespoon
- Cayenne – 2 tablespoons
- Salt – 1 tablespoon
- Black pepper – 2 tablespoons

The Filling

- Chopped onion – 1 cup
- Garlic – 5 cloves
- Thyme – 5 sprigs

Directions:

Place chicken in brine overnight.

Combine the rub ingredients & Rub the chicken with the spice mixture then fill the cavity with chopped onion, garlic, and thyme.

Smoke the chicken for approximately 3 hours.

12. Sweet Honey Smoked Brown Turkey

Ingredients:

- Whole Turkey (6-lbs., 2.7-kg.)
- Salt – 5 tablespoons
- Brown sugar – 5 tablespoons
- Thyme – 1 tablespoon
- Chopped rosemary – 1 tablespoon
- Sage – 1 tablespoon
- Black pepper – 2 $\frac{1}{2}$ teaspoons
- Garlic powder – 2 teaspoons
- Raw honey – 1 cup
- Brown sugar – 3 tablespoons
- Apple Cider Vinegar – 2 tablespoons

- Mustard – $\frac{3}{4}$ tablespoon
- Salt - 1 teaspoon
- Pepper – 2 teaspoons

Directions:

Combine the rub ingredients & Rub the turkey with the spice mixture then let it rest for a few minutes.

Smoke the turkey for approximately 4 hours.

Quickly place brown sugar, apple cider vinegar, mustard, salt, and pepper in a bowl then pour raw honey over the mixture. Stir until combined.

Baste the smoked turkey with the honey mixture then return it to the Smoker.

13. Spicy Smoked Chicken Garlic

Ingredients:

- Whole Chicken (3-lbs., 1.4-kg.)
- Salt – 1 teaspoon
- Paprika – 1 teaspoon
- Garlic powder – 1 ½ teaspoons
- Black pepper – 1 ½ teaspoons
- Red chili flakes – 2 teaspoons
- Cayenne pepper – ½ teaspoon
- Thyme – ¾ teaspoon
- Oregano – ½ teaspoon
- Brown sugar – 3 tablespoons

Directions:

Rub the chicken with salt, paprika, garlic powder, black pepper, red chili flakes, cayenne pepper, thyme, oregano, and brown sugar.

Wrap the seasoned chicken with plastic wrap then let it rest for approximately an hour. Store in the fridge to keep it fresh

Smoke the chicken for approximately 3 hours.

Cut the smoked chicken into pieces then serve.

14. Hot Smoked Shredded Chicken

Ingredients:

- Boneless Chicken breast (3-lbs., 1.4-kg.)
- Paprika – 3 tablespoons
- Chili powder – 3 tablespoons
- Thyme – 1 ½ tablespoons
- Garlic powder – 1 ½ tablespoons
- Onion powder – 1 ½ tablespoons
- Cayenne – 3 tablespoons
- Salt – 1 ½ tablespoons
- Black pepper – 1 ½ tablespoons

- Honey – $\frac{1}{2}$ cup
- Maple syrup – $\frac{1}{4}$ cup
- Brown sugar – 2 tablespoons

Directions:

Combine the rub ingredients and rub with the spice mixture. Let it rest for a few minutes.

Smoke the chicken for an hour then transfer to a disposable aluminum pan.

Quickly combine honey with maple syrup then stir until incorporated.

Drizzle half of the honey mixture over the chicken breast then sprinkle brown sugar on top.

Place the disposable aluminum pan with chicken inside in the Pellet smoker then smoke for about 2 hours.

15. White Smoked Chicken Breast

Ingredients:

- Boneless Chicken breast (4.5-lbs., 2 -kg.)
- Vegetable oil – 3 tablespoons
- Chicken broth – ¼ cup
- Worcestershire sauce – 2 tablespoons
- Salt – ¾ tablespoon
- Garlic powder – 1 ½ teaspoons
- Onion powder – 1 ½ teaspoons
- Bay leaf – ¾ teaspoon
- Thyme – ¾ teaspoon
- Sage – ¾ teaspoon

- Black pepper – $\frac{3}{4}$ teaspoon
- Salt – 2 tablespoons
- Minced garlic – 3 tablespoons
- Minced ginger – 1 tablespoon
- Lemon juice – 3 tablespoons

Directions:

Pour vegetable oil and chicken broth into a bowl then season with Worcestershire sauce, salt, garlic powder, onion powder, bay leaf, thyme, sage, and black pepper. Stir the liquid until incorporated.

Fill an injector with the liquid mixture then inject the chicken breast at several places.

After that, combine the rub ingredients & Rub the chicken breast with the spice mixture then let it rest for an hour.

Smoke the chicken for 2 hours.

16. Barbecue Chicken

Ingredients:

- 8 Chicken breasts
- Two t. salt
- Two c. barbecue sauce, divided
- Two t. garlic powder
- Two t. pepper

Directions:

Add Preferred Wood Pellet pellets to your smoker and follow your cooker's startup procedure. Preheat your smoker, with your lid closed, until it reaches 250.

Rub the chicken with the spices and lay in a roasting pan. Cover the chicken before placing them on the grill. For about two hours, let them smoke. It should reach 165. During the last 15 minutes, baste with a c. of barbecue sauce.

Serve with the rest of the sauce.

17. Whole Turkey

Ingredients:

- Two t. thyme
- Two t. sage
- ½ c. apple juice
- One stick melted butter
- ¼ c. poultry seasoning
- 10-12-pound turkey

Directions:

Add Preferred Wood Pellet pellets to your smoker and follow your cooker's startup procedure. Preheat your smoker, with your lid closed, until it reaches 250.

Rub the oil and seasoning on the turkey. Get some in under the skin as well as inside.

Mix the thyme, sage, juice, and butter.

Place the turkey in a roasting pan, put it on the grill, cover, and cook 5-6 hours. Baste it every hour with the juice mixture. It should reach 165. Let it rest for 15-20 minutes before carving.

18. Barbecue Chicken Breasts

Ingredients:

- Two T. Worcestershire sauce
- ½ c. hot barbecue sauce
- One c. barbecue sauce
- Two cloves minced garlic
- ¼ c. olive oil
- 4 chicken breasts

Directions:

Put the chicken breasts into a deep container.

In another bowl, put the Worcestershire sauce, barbecue sauces, garlic, and olive oil. Stir well to combine.

Use half to marinate the chicken and reserve the rest for basting.

Add Preferred Wood Pellet pellets to your smoker and follow your cooker's startup procedure. Preheat your smoker, with your lid closed, until it reaches 350.

Take the chicken breasts out of the sauce. On the grill, place them before smoking them for approximately 20 minutes.

About ten minutes before the chicken is finished, baste with reserved barbecue sauce.

19. Cilantro-Lime Chicken

Ingredients:

- Pepper
- Salt
- 4 cloves minced garlic
- $\frac{1}{2}$ c. lime juice
- One c. honey
- Two T. olive oil
- $\frac{1}{2}$ c. chopped cilantro
- 4 chicken breasts

Directions:

Put the chicken breasts into a large zip-top bag.

In another bowl, put the pepper, salt, olive oil, garlic, honey, lime juice, and cilantro. Stir well to combine.

Use half as a marinade and reserve the rest for later.

Place into the refrigerator for four to five hours.

Remove the chicken breasts the bag. Use paper towels to pat them dry. Let them smoke up in the grill for about fifteen mins.

About five minutes before the chicken is finished, baste with reserved marinade.

20. Lemon Honey Chicken

Ingredients:

- Pepper
- Salt
- Chopped rosemary
- One clove crushed garlic
- One T. honey
- Juice of one lemon
- $\frac{1}{2}$ c. chicken broth
- 3 T. butter
- 4 chicken breasts

Directions:

Place a pan on the stove and melt the butter. Place chicken breasts into hot butter and sear on each side until a nice color has formed.

Take out of the pan and allow resting for ten minutes.

In a small bowl, put the pepper, salt, rosemary, garlic, honey, lemon juice, and broth. Stir well to combine.

Rub each breast with the honey lemon mixture.

Put the chicken breasts onto the preheated grill and grill for 20 minutes.

21. Herbed Coffee Chicken

Ingredients:

- Salt
- $\frac{3}{4}$ c. strong brewed coffee
- One t. coriander seeds
- 4 lemon slices
- One t. peppercorns
- One t. mustard seeds
- $\frac{1}{2}$ c. chicken broth
- $\frac{1}{4}$ c. dark brown sugar, packed
- Two T. melted butter

- 4 chicken breast halves

Directions:

Rub the butter on the chicken and rub in the salt.

In an enormous container, stir together the remaining ingredients. Cover the chicken with marinade.

Place into the refrigerator for two hours.

Add Preferred Wood Pellet pellets to your smoker and follow your cooker's startup procedure. Preheat your smoker, with your lid closed, until it reaches 350.

Smoke the chicken for ten minutes. There is no need to flip. Serve.

22. Red Pepper Chicken Thighs

Ingredients:

- One T. garlic powder
- One t. curry powder
- One t. red pepper flakes
- One t. black pepper
- Two T. olive oil
- ½ c. chicken broth
- One t. oregano
- One t. paprika
- Two pounds chicken thighs

Directions:

Put the chicken thighs into a large flat dish in a single layer.

In a bowl, put the olive oil, garlic powder, curry, oregano, pepper, paprika, red pepper flakes, and broth. Stir well to combine.

The mixture should be poured on top of the chicken.

Let the chicken marinate for four hours.

Add Preferred Wood Pellet pellets to your smoker and follow your cooker's startup procedure. Preheat your smoker, with your lid closed, until it reaches 450.

The chicken thighs should be removed from the bag. Use paper towels to pat them dry. Place them onto the preheated grill with the skin down and smoke for ten minutes. Turnover and cook for an additional ten minutes.

23. Candied Smoked Salmon with Orange Ginger Rub

Ingredients:

- Salmon fillet (4-lbs., 1.8-kg.)

The Marinade

- Brown sugar – ¼ cup
- Salt – ½ teaspoon

The Rub

- Minced garlic – 2 tablespoons
- Grated fresh ginger – 1 teaspoon

- Grated orange zest – $\frac{1}{2}$ teaspoon
- Cayenne pepper – $\frac{1}{2}$ teaspoon

The Glaze

- Red wine – 2 tablespoons
- Dark rum – 2 tablespoons
- Brown sugar – 1 $\frac{1}{2}$ cups
- Honey – 1 cup

Directions:

Mix salt with brown sugar then apply over the salmon fillet.

Rub the salmon fillet with the spice mixture then set aside.

Place the seasoned salmon in Pellet smoker and smoke for 2 hours.

Mix red wine with dark rum, brown sugar, and honey then stir until dissolved. Baste.

24. Juicy Lime Smoked Tuna Belly

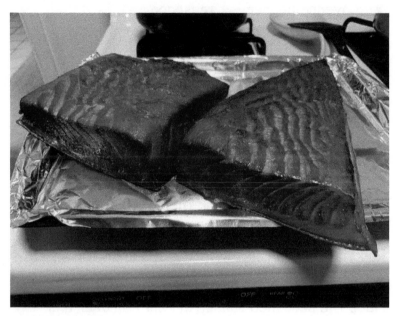

Ingredients:

- Tuna belly (3-lb., 1.4-kg.)
- The Marinade
- Fresh limes – 2
- White sugar – 2 tablespoons
- Brown sugar – 3 tablespoons
- Pepper – $\frac{1}{2}$ teaspoon
- Soy sauce – 1 tablespoon
- Sriracha sauce – 2 tablespoons

Directions:

Marinate the tuna belly with the juice for 10 minutes.

Meanwhile, combine white sugar with brown sugar, pepper, soy sauce, and Sriracha sauce then mix well.

Wash and rinse the tuna belly then pat it dry.

Wait until the Pellet smoker reaches the desired Smoke Temperature then place the seasoned tuna belly in it.

Smoke the tuna belly for 2 hours or until it flakes and once it is done, remove it from the Smoker.

25. Lemon Butter Smoked Mackerel with Juniper Berries Brine

Ingredients:

- Mackerel fillet (4-lbs., 1.8-kg.)

The Brine

- Cold water – 4 cups
- Mustard seeds – 1 tablespoon
- Dried juniper berries – 1 tablespoon
- Bay leaves – 3
- Salt – 1 tablespoon

The Glaze

- Butter – 2 tablespoons

- Lemon juice – 2 tablespoons

Directions:

Pour cold water into a container then season with salt, bay leaves, dried juniper berries, and mustard seeds then stir well.

Add the mackerel fillet to the brine mixture then soak. Place the salted mackerel on a sheet of aluminum foil then baste butter over it.

Drizzle lemon juice then wrap the mackerel fillet with the aluminum foil.

Smoke the wrapped mackerel for 2 hours or until it flakes and once it is done, remove from the Smoker.

26. Smoked Crab

Ingredients:

- Fresh Crabs (7-lb., 3.2-kg.)

The Sauce

- Salt – 1 tablespoon
- Cayenne pepper – 1 $\frac{1}{2}$ teaspoons
- Salted butter – 2 cups
- Lemon juice – $\frac{1}{2}$ cup
- Worcestershire sauce – 1 tablespoon
- Garlic powder – 2 teaspoons
- Smoked paprika – 2 teaspoons

Directions:

Preheat a saucepan over low heat then melt the butter. Let it cool.

Season the melted butter with salt, cayenne pepper, Worcestershire sauce, garlic powder, and smoked paprika then pour lemon juice into the melted butter. Stir until incorporated and set aside.

Arrange the crabs in a disposable aluminum pan then drizzle the sauce over the crabs.

Smoke the crabs for 30 minutes then remove from the Smoker.

27. Cayenne Garlic Smoked Shrimp

Ingredients:

- Fresh Shrimps (3-lb., 1.4-kg.)

The Spices

- Olive oil – 2 tablespoons
- Lemon juice – 2 tablespoons
- Salt – $\frac{3}{4}$ teaspoon
- Smoked paprika – 2 teaspoons
- Pepper – $\frac{1}{2}$ teaspoon
- Garlic powder – 2 tablespoons
- Onion powder – 2 tablespoons
- Dried thyme – 1 teaspoon
- Cayenne pepper – 2 teaspoons

Directions:

Combine salt, smoked paprika, pepper, garlic powder, onion powder, dried thyme, and cayenne pepper then mix well. Set aside.

Drizzle olive oil and lemon juice over the shrimps and shake to coat. Let the shrimps rest for approximately 5 minutes.

Sprinkle the spice mixture over the shrimps then stir until the shrimps are entirely seasoned.

Place the disposable aluminum pan with shrimps in the Pellet smoker and smoke the shrimps for 15 minutes. The shrimps will be opaque and pink.

Remove the smoked shrimps from the Pellet smoker and transfer to a serving dish.

Serve and enjoy.

28. Cinnamon Ginger Smoked Crab

Ingredients:

- Fresh Crabs (7-lb., 3.2-kg.)

The Spices

- Salt – 1 tablespoon
- Ground celery seeds – 3 tablespoons
- Ground mustard – 2 teaspoons
- Cayenne pepper – ½ teaspoon
- Black pepper – ½ teaspoon
- Smoked paprika – 1 ½ teaspoons
- Ground clove – A pinch
- Ground allspice – ¾ teaspoon

- Ground ginger – 1 teaspoon
- Ground cardamom – ½ teaspoon
- Ground cinnamon – ½ teaspoon
- Bay leaves - 2

Directions:

Combine the whole spices & Sprinkle the spice mixture over the crabs then wrap the crabs with aluminum foil.

Place the wrapped crabs in the Pellet smoker and smoke for 30 minutes.

Once it is done, remove the wrapped smoked carbs from the Pellet smoker and let it rest for approximately 10 minutes.

Unwrap the smoked crabs and transfer it to a serving dish.

29. Simple Grilled Oysters

Ingredients:
- 4 dozen oysters, scrubbed
- Lemon wedges
- 1 C butter
- 1 Tsp seasoned salt
- 1 tsp lemon pepper

Directions:

Preheat pellet grill to 350F.

Melt butter with seasoned salt and lemon pepper, mixing well. Simmer 10 minutes.

Place oysters, unshelled, on pellet grill.

When shells pop open (3-5 minutes), use an oyster knife to detach oyster from top shell, and plop it back into the cup with the hot oyster liquor. Discard the lid.

Add a teaspoon of seasoned butter and serve.

30. Garlic Asiago Oysters

Ingredients:

- 1 lb. sweet cream butter
- 1 Tbsp. minced garlic
- 2 dozen fresh oysters
- $\frac{1}{2}$ C. grated Asiago cheese
- French bread, warmed
- $\frac{1}{4}$ cup chives, diced

Directions:

Start pellet grill and heat to medium high.

Melt butter over medium-high heat. Reduce heat to low and stir in garlic.

Cook 1 minute and remove from heat.

Place oysters, cup down, on pellet grill. As soon as shells pop open, remove from grill.

Shuck oysters, keeping as much of the oyster liquor in place as possible.

Cut connective muscle and return each oyster to its shell.

Drizzle each oyster with 2 teaspoons butter mixture and sprinkle with 1 teaspoon cheese. Grill over high heat 3 minutes or until cheese browns. Sprinkle with chives.

Remove from pellet grill and serve immediately with bread and remaining butter on the side.

31. Wasabi Oysters

Ingredients:

- 12 small Pacific oysters, raw in shell 2 Tbsp. white wine vinegar

- 8 oz white wine 1/4 C shallots, minced

- 2 Tbsp. wasabi mustard 1 Tbsp. soy sauce

- 1 C unsalted butter, cubed 1 C chopped cilantro leaves

- Salt and black pepper to taste

Directions:

In a saucepan, over medium heat, combine the white wine vinegar, wine, and shallots. Simmer until the liquid is slightly reduced. Add wasabi mustard and soy sauce, stirring.

Over low heat gradually whisks in butter. Do not let the mixture boil. stir in cilantro, and remove from heat.

Cook oysters until shells just open. Remove oysters from the pellet grill and cut the connective muscle from the top shell,

Press each oyster (in shell) into the coarse salt to keep it upright, then spoon 1-2 teaspoons of wasabi-butter sauce over each and serve immediately.

32. Fish Camp Trout

Ingredients:

- 4 small whole trout, cleaned
- 4 strips of bacon
- 4 sprigs of fresh thyme
- 1 lemon
- salt and pepper to taste

Directions:

Oil grates and preheat pellet grill. Fry bacon, so that it is started to cook, but is still soft. Rinse out the trout and pat dry with a paper towel.

Place a sprig of thyme inside each fish. Wrap each trout with a strip of bacon and secure with a toothpick.

Place trout on pellet grill or in an oiled grill basket, and grill 5-7 minutes per side depending on the size of the trout. The trout is done when the meat turns opaque in the center and easily flakes.

Squeeze a little fresh lemon juice over each fish and serve.

33. Southern-Grilled Bass

Ingredients:

- 2 lbs. bass fillets or steaks
- 1 C. mayonnaise
- 4 oz. soy sauce

Directions:

Mix mayonnaise and soy sauce.

Cover entire surface (meat side) of each bass fillet with mixture.

Place on pellet grill, skin-side down. Do not turn.

When edges turn up and scales flake, remove and serve.

34. Pacific Northwest Salmon with Lemon Dill Sauce

Ingredients:

- 6lb Chinook salmon fillets
- Salt to taste
- 1 C butter, melted
- 1 C lemon juice
- 4 Tbsp. dried dill weed
- 1 Tbsp. garlic salt
- Black pepper to taste
- 4 C plain yogurt

Directions:

Place salmon fillets in a baking dish.

Mix the butter and 1/2 lemon juice in a small bowl, and drizzle over the salmon. Season with salt & pepper.

Combine yogurt, dill, garlic powder, sea salt, and pepper. Spread sauce evenly over salmon.

Quickly wipe hot pellet grill grate with a towel dipped in a little canola oil, place fillets on grill, tent with foil, and close lid.

Grill fish, skin down, to medium rare, about 6 minutes.

35. Seared Wasabi Tuna

Ingredients:

- 6-ounce tuna steaks
- 1 1/4 cup white wine
- 1 cup cilantro leaves
- 1 cup unsalted butter
- 1/4 cup shallots, minced
- 2 Tbsp. white wine vinegar
- 1 tablespoon wasabi paste
- 1 tablespoon soy sauce
- 1 tablespoon olive oil
- salt and pepper to taste

Directions:

Combine wine, wine vinegar and shallots in a saucepan over medium heat. Simmer to reduce to about 2 tablespoons. Strain out the shallots and discard.

Add wasabi and soy sauce to mixture and reduce Preferred Wood Pellet. Slowly add butter while stirring until thoroughly mixed. Stir in cilantro and remove from heat. Set aside.

Brush tuna steaks with olive oil. Season with salt and pepper and place on grill.

Grill for 90 seconds then turn and continue grilling for 90 seconds more.

36. Bacon Grilled Crappie

Ingredients:

- 20 Crappie Fillets
- 20 Bacon Slices
- $\frac{1}{4}$ teaspoon garlic powder
- $\frac{1}{4}$ teaspoon onion powder
- $\frac{1}{4}$ teaspoon pepper

Directions:

Sprinkle spices on fillets. Roll up fillets, wrap with bacon and peg with a toothpick.

Grill over meager heat, with apple Preferred Wood Pellet pellets, turning fillets several times.

Be sure to put out all flames caused by bacon grease with a water spray bottle.

Cook until bacon is brown and inside of fillet flakes.

37. Mojo Shrimp Skewer Appetizers

Ingredients:

- 2 lbs. sliced bacon
- 64 raw prawns, tail off
- 2 C Traditional Cuban Mojo
- $\frac{1}{4}$ C Adobo Criollo
- 32 Preferred Wood Pellet skewers, soaked

Directions:

Rinse raw prawns and drain. In a large bowl, toss prawns and Adobo Criollo spices.

Wrap each prawn in $\frac{1}{2}$ slice of bacon, and thread two wraps onto each skewer, touching, and with skewer through both the bacon and the shrimp.

Bring pellet grill to medium heat, oil, and lay skewers in grill.

Grill 3-5 minutes, until bacon is cooked, flip, and cook 2-3 more minutes.

Remove from grill and let rest on a paper-towel covered platters 2-3 minutes before serving. for this type of grilling.

38. Sweet Grilled Lobster Tails

Ingredients:

- 12 lobster tails
- ½ C olive oil
- ¼ C fresh lemon juice
- ½ C butter
- 1 Tbsp. crushed garlic
- 1 tsp sugar
- 1/2 tsp salt
- ½ tsp black pepper

Directions:

Combine lemon juice, butter, garlic, salt, and pepper over med-low heat and mix until well blended, keep warm.

Create a "cool zone" at one end of the pellet grill. Brush the meat side of tails with olive oil, place onto grill and cook for 5-7 minutes, depending on the size of the lobster tail.

After turning, baste meat with garlic butter 2-3 times.

The shell should be bright red when they are finished. Remove the tails from the grill, and using large kitchen shears, cut the top part of the shell open.

Serve with warm garlic butter for dipping.

39. Seasoned Smoked Oysters

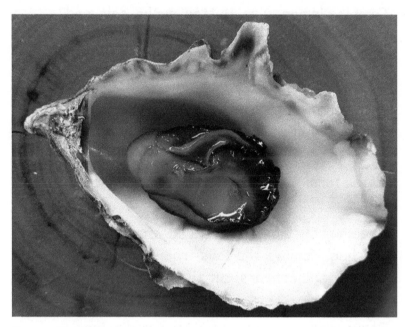

Ingredients:

- ½ cup soy sauce
- 2 tablespoons Worcestershire sauce
- 1 cup firmly packed brown sugar
- 2 dried bay leaves
- 2 garlic cloves, minced
- 2 teaspoons salt and black pepper
- 1 tablespoon hot sauce
- 1 tablespoon onion powder
- 2 dozen raw, shucked oysters
- ¼ cup olive oil

- $\frac{1}{2}$ cup (1 stick) unsalted butter
- 1 teaspoon garlic powder

Directions:

In a large container, mix the water, soy sauce, Worcestershire, salt, sugar, bay leaves, garlic, pepper, hot sauce, and onion powder.

Submerge the raw oysters in the brine and refrigerate overnight.

Place the oysters on a non-stick grill mat, drizzle with the olive oil, and place the mat in the smoker.

Smoke the oysters for $1\frac{1}{2}$ to 2 hours, until firm. Serve with the butter and garlic powder.

40. Sugar-Crusted Red Snapper

Ingredients:

- 1 tablespoon brown sugar
- 2 teaspoons minced garlic
- 2 teaspoons salt
- 2 teaspoons freshly ground black pepper
- $\frac{1}{2}$ teaspoon crushed red pepper flakes
- 1 (1$\frac{1}{2}$- to 2-pound) red snapper fillet
- 2 tablespoons olive oil, plus more for oiling the grate
- 1 sliced lime, for garnish

Directions:

Following the manufacturer's specific start-up procedure, preheat the smoker to 225°F, and add alder Preferred Wood Pellet.

In a small bowl, mix the brown sugar, garlic, and salt, pepper, and red pepper flakes to make a spice blend.

Rub the olive oil all over the fish and apply the spice blend to coat.

Oil the grill grate or a nonstick grill mat or perforated pizza screen. Place the fillet on the smoker rack and smoke for 1 to $1\frac{1}{2}$ hours, until the internal Smoke Temperature registers 145°F.

Remove the fish from Preferred Wood Pellet and serve hot with the lime slices.

41. Peppercorn-Dill Mahi-Mahi

Ingredients:

- 4 mahi-mahi fillets
- $\frac{1}{4}$ cup chopped fresh dill
- 2 tablespoons freshly squeezed lemon juice
- 1 tablespoon crushed black peppercorns
- 2 teaspoons minced garlic
- 1 teaspoon onion powder
- 1 teaspoon salt
- 2 tablespoons olive oil

Directions:

Trim the fillets as needed, cutting out any visible red bloodline. It will not hurt you, but its more robust flavor can quickly permeate the rest of the fillet.

In a small bowl, whisk together the dill, lemon juice, peppercorns, garlic, onion powder, and salt to make a seasoning.

Rub the fish with the olive oil and apply the seasoning all over. Oil the grill grate or a nonstick grill mat or perforated pizza screen.

Place the fillets on the smoker rack and smoke for 1 to $1\frac{1}{2}$ hours.

42. Fish Tacos with Fiery Peppers

Ingredients:

- 1 (16-ounce) carton prepared sweet coleslaw
- 1 small red onion, chopped
- 1 poblano pepper, chopped
- 1 jalapeño pepper, chopped
- 1 serrano pepper, chopped
- $\frac{1}{4}$ cup chopped fresh cilantro
- 1 tablespoon minced garlic
- 2 teaspoons salt, divided
- 2 teaspoons freshly ground black pepper, divided

- 1 lime, halved
- 1-pound skinless cod, halibut, or any white fish (see tip)
- 1 tablespoon olive oil, plus more for oiling the grate
- Flour or corn tortillas
- 1 avocado, sliced thin

Directions:

Make the slaw.

Juice one half of the lime and cut the other half into wedges. Rub the fish all over with the lime juice and olive oil.

Season the fish & Place the fish on the smoker rack and smoke for 1 to $1\frac{1}{2}$ hours

43. Honey-Cayenne Sea Scallops

Ingredients:

- $\frac{1}{2}$ cup (1 stick) butter, melted
- $\frac{1}{4}$ cup honey
- 2 tablespoons ground cayenne pepper
- 1 tablespoon brown sugar
- 1 teaspoon garlic powder
- 1 teaspoon onion powder
- $\frac{1}{2}$ teaspoon salt
- 20 sea scallops (about 2 pounds)

Directions:

In a small bowl, whisk together the butter, honey, cayenne, brown sugar, garlic powder, onion powder, and salt.

Place the scallops in a disposable aluminum foil roasting pan and pour the seasoned honey butter over them.

Set the pan on the smoker rack and smoke the scallops for about 25 minutes, until opaque and firm and the internal Smoke Temperature registers 130°F.

Remove the scallops from Preferred Wood Pellet and serve hot.

44. Lemon Butter Lobster Tails

Ingredients:

- 4 (8-ounce) lobster tails, fresh (not frozen)
- 1 cup (2 sticks) unsalted butter, melted, divided
- Juice of 2 lemons
- 1 teaspoon minced garlic
- 1 teaspoon dried thyme
- 1 teaspoon dried rosemary
- 1 teaspoon salt
- 1 teaspoon freshly ground black pepper
- Olive oil, for oiling the grate
- $\frac{1}{4}$ cup chopped fresh parsley

Directions:

In a small bowl, whisk together the butter, lemon juice, garlic, thyme, rosemary, salt, and pepper. Baste each lobster tail with 1 tablespoon of lemon butter.

Place the tails on the smoker rack split-side up.

Smoke the tails for 45 minutes to 1 hour, basting each with 1 tablespoon of lemon butter once during cooking.

Remove the lobster tails & sprinkle with the parsley and serve with the remaining lemon butter for dipping.

45. Smoked Fresh Salmon fillets

Ingredients:

- 1 Salmon fillets (fresh, wild, skin on)
- 1/3 Teaspoon of Old Bay Seasoning
- 1 Teaspoon of Basic Seafood Seasoning

Directions:

Pepping for the Grill

Wash salmon fillets fish with cold water and use a paper towel to pat dry

Rub the seasoning on the salmon fillets lightly

Pepping on the Preferred Wood Pellet smoker

Set the Preferred Wood Pellet smoker grill to indirect cooking and preheat to 400°F

Place the fillets skin down directly on the grill grates

Smoke the salmon fillets in the smoker until the internal Smoke Temperature rises to 140°F and fork can easily flake the flesh

Allow the salmon resting for 5 minutes

Serve and enjoy

46. Caribbean Smoked Rockfish

Ingredients:

- 4 Ounces of Pacific Rockfish fillets
- 1 Tablespoon of Caribbean seafood seasoning
- 2 Teaspoons of extra virgin olive oil

Directions:

Rub olive oil to all sides of the rockfish fillets

Rub the seasoning on the salmon fillets lightly

Place the fillets skin down directly on the grill grates

Smoke the salmon fillets in the smoker until the internal Smoke Temperature rises to 140°F and fork can easily flake the flesh

Allow the salmon resting for 5 minutes

Serve and enjoy

47. Smoked Shrimp Tilapia

Ingredients:

- 3 Ounces Tilapia fillets (fresh, farmed)
- 3/4 Teaspoon of Paprika (smoked)
- 1 Tablespoon of extra virgin olive
- 3/4 Teaspoon of Seafood Seasoning

Ingredients for Shrimp Stuffing:

- 1/2 Pound of Tail-off Shrimp
- 1/2 Cup of Breadcrumbs
- 1/2 Tablespoon of salted Butter
- 3/4 Teaspoon of pepper
- 1 Egg (small, beaten)

- 1/4 Cup of mayonnaise
- 3/4 Teaspoon of Parsley (dried)

Directions:

Pour shrimps into a food processor to chop it finely

Heat olive over medium-high heat in a large skillet, adds butter and melts it, and adds onion and sauté until soft

Combine sautéed mixture, shrimp and the remaining ingredients in a bowl that has cover

Rub olive oil on all sides of the fillets. Use a spoon to stuff some great stuffing on the back of each fillet.

Spread the stuffing on the back of the fillets

Fold the tilapia fillets into twos and use toothpicks to hold them tight.

Roast the fillets for 40 minutes

48. Smoked Brined Tuna

Ingredients:

- 3 Pounds of Salmon fillets (farmed)
- 2 Cups of Fresh fish Brine

Directions:

Cut the fillets into 4 inches sizes so to be able to cook at an equal rate

Put the pork chops into a sealable plastic container and pour into the container Fresh fish Brine

Cover it and place in the fridge overnight

After this duration remove the pork chops and pat dry with paper towels

Set the Smoker grill to indirect cooking

Transfer the salmon fillets into Teflon-coated fiberglass mat

Preheat the smoker to 180°F and cook until the internal Smoke Temperature of the salmon fillets rises to 145°F

49. Smoked Sauced Tuna

Ingredients:

- 10 Ounces Tuna Steaks (fresh)
- 1 Cup of Teriyaki sauce

Directions:

Cut the tuna into 4 inches sizes so to be able to cook at an equal rate

Put the tuna steaks into a sealable plastic container and pour into the container Teriyaki sauce

Cover it and place in the fridge for 3 hours

After this duration remove the tuna steaks and pat dry with paper towels

Transfer the fillet to nonstick grill tray and place in the smoker for 1 hour

After this time increase Preferred Wood Pellet to 250°F and cook until the internal Smoke Temperature of the tuna rises to 145°F

Remove them from the grill and allow resting for 10 minutes

Serve and enjoy

50. Smoked Brined Trout

Ingredients:

- 2 Whole Trout (fresh, skin on, pin bones removed)
- 3 Cups of Fresh fish Brine

Directions:

Put the trout into a sealable plastic container and pour into the container Fresh fish Brine

Transfer the fillet to nonstick grill tray and place in the smoker for 1 minute

Continue smoking until the internal he of the tuna rises to 145°F

Remove them from the smoker and allow resting for 5 minutes

Serve and enjoy

CONCLUSION

So now that we have reached the end of the book, I am very optimistic that you are well acquainted with some of the finest smoker grill recipes which will make you a pro at grilling, BBQ, and cooking in general.

Sometimes seeing so many recipes briefly can be very overwhelming. Therefore we had segmented this book into different sections each spanning recipes of a similar kind. So, go through the book as and when needed and make sure to follow the instructions in the recipe thoroughly.